S124

ZONE : ZERO

AHSAHTA PRESS

The New Series

NUMBER 24

ZONE : ZERO

STEPHANIE STRICKLAND

AHSAHTA PRESS

BOISE STATE UNIVERSITY • BOISE • IDAHO • 2008

Ahsahta Press, Boise State University
Boise, Idaho 83725
http://ahsahtapress.boisestate.edu

Printed in the United States of America
Cover design by Quemadura
Book design by Janet Holmes
First printing September 2008
ISBN-13: 978-1-934103-01-2

Library of Congress Cataloging-in-Publication Data
Strickland, Stephanie.
Zone : zero / Stephanie Strickland.
p. cm. -- (The new series ; no. 24)
Includes bibliographical references.
ISBN-13: 978-1-934103-01-2 (pbk. : alk. paper)
ISBN-10: 1-934103-01-2 (pbk. : alk. paper)
I. Title.
PS3569.T69543Z43 2008
811'.54--DC22

2007047288

ACKNOWLEDGMENTS

Thanks to the editors and publications that published these poems in this form or another: *American Letters & Commentary*, "Absinthe 9: Colette" (as "Colette"); *Bird Dog*, "slippingglimpse"; *Black Clock*, "Where Geography Stops,"; *Boston Review*, "Ballad of Sand and Harry Soot"; *Chain*, "Gibbous Statement"; *Chelsea*, "Absinthe 2: Pillar" (as "Pillar"), "Absinthe 7: Ecstasy" (as "Ecstasy"); *Colorado Review*, "Prisoner in the Cave"; *Columbia Poetry Review*, "Absinthe 1: *I*," "Absinthe 8: Rabi'a," "Absinthe 10: Amma," "Occam and Miranda"; *Connecticut Review*, "Sierra Madre," "20/21 Vision"; *Court Green*, "Absinthe 3: Patti," "Constant Quiet," "Stone Barn"; *Critiphoria*, "To Gödel"; *Drunken Boat*, "Absinthe 11: Enormous Washerwomen on Stilts," "Prisoner in the Tower"; *Electronic Poetry Review*, "Versus Vega: Precessing"; *Fence*, "War Day"; *Furtherfield Net Behavior Residency*, "Versus Vega: Precessing" (digital); *Hyperrhiz: New Media Cultures*, "slippingglimpse" (digital); *Image: A Journal of the Arts and Religion*, "The Interior Castle"; *jubilat*, "Absinthe 5: Apollinaria-Dorotheus" (as "Quiet"); *Lumina*, "Open Cage" (as "Loss in an Open Cage"); *Meridian*, "X-Ray Eyes"; *Poetry New York*, "Islands (Invaginated by Saltwater . . ." (as "Islands Invaginated by Saltwater . . ."); *Word Circuits Gallery*, "The Ballad of Sand and Harry Soot" (digital).

"Absinthe 11: Enormous Washerwomen on Stilts" and "Prisoner in the Tower" were finalists in *Drunken Boat*'s PanLiterary Awards.

"At Auden's Museum" previously appeared in *The Muse Strikes Back: A Poetic Response by Women to Men*, Story Line Press, 1997.

"Ballad of Sand and Harry Soot" received the 2nd Annual Poetry Award from *Boston Review*.

"electrical disturbances propagate through space as" and "Survey" previously appeared in *A Sing Economy*, Flim Forum Press, 2008.

Special thanks to the Corporation of Yaddo for its generosity and support during the writing of this book.

Contents

ZONE MOTE ELSE

NOTES

CD

Ballad of Sand and Harry Soot (digital)
slippingglimpse (digital)

ZONE : ZERO

We forget that we must always return to zero
in order to pass from one word to the next.

—John Cage, *For the Birds*

ZONE ARMORY WAR

constant quiet
        intercostal
                intercoastal green & silver
                muscled gillflesh slipping into
        opens out of
constant quiet

constant quiet
        Mississippi
                overflowing built a levee
                longer higher than the Great
        Wall of China
constant quiet

constant quiet
        building building
                horse paunch pistol man
                long back cropper convict
        steel muscled
constant quiet

constant quiet
        longer higher
                than the Great Wall of China
                Egypt Mississippi hunger
      flogged
constant quiet

constant quiet
        storm of air
               ocean storms
               River rising
      field gone train gone man gone
constant quiet

constant quiet
        who can open
              who can
              hold it
      constant
quiet

Lost in a cave of warm, wavering stream pumped through projectors
overhead, we saw floaters, drift, motes eddying, a beam—
but more vividly, onscreen, the not
quite there body bruised by wind: a heroine;
the hero's bear-skin
coat, his bear-grease hair; moving
shadows, spooling
silver;

&

then bound, to video
screens, all flesh a tone between
purple and green, we
forgot
daylight, dusk, a path where someone not
quite seen waits, where rain muzzles the light, where white
silk slips
to slivered mist as darkness falls, deep
pleats of a cloak
thrown down by the king stooped
to kneel in the live
wood; we

see

no king. We are turning our attention
to that slim
man, his tattooed hair, alloyed skin. Pierced
with sensors, miked, his garb
a sheath of wireless wires twining
his body like snakes that feed at
the flashing towers, he is
rippling inside
his aura of amperes,
idling, on,

almost gone—
booting
up://

rubble Deep Field every quarter square degree
of sky a moonsworth : probing (counting   mirroring . . .)
"discovers"

All   iron anywhere aluminum vanadium Orange trees

in the universe   Matter   less
than one tenth-of-one
per

/ cent

. . . Dominance of dark : Sloan survey at Sunspot
rogue infernos coiled wheels making up
time   the starry SFX

dominantly

dark :
so it is written   faint
hiss of tumblers as the safe cracks

rare and *threatened*

numbed by prevalence   quintillions   *bio-*
devour   not a bomb
a hailed brother

over

whelmed
thin
dime

<table>
<tr>
<td>

holy war
to keep the sun moving a sacrifice
process jaw jaw
mother sweep the floor

</td>
<td></td>
</tr>
<tr>
<td></td>
<td>

never go anywhere bliss so much
flows by
not sea or sky no
woman no cry

</td>
</tr>
<tr>
<td>

mystic immersion
enabled
smite embedding
enabled

</td>
<td></td>
</tr>
<tr>
<td></td>
<td>

on deck before he didn't
know it death
old
football yarns

</td>
</tr>
<tr>
<td>

so tensely forgot
Plum Creek to Plum Island
spent
fuel rocks

</td>
<td></td>
</tr>
<tr>
<td></td>
<td>

the green and white
alabaster
city of ancient glowing
lamps

</td>
</tr>
<tr>
<td>

pyre at the river
ember-eyed stranger
strangling
net of his abundant hair

</td>
<td></td>
</tr>
<tr>
<td></td>
<td>

cartoons graphing
statistics
videophone . . . lag . . . br eak
 i ng up

</td>
</tr>
</table>

Discovery Channel gladiator slave awarded wooden freedom sword refusing it to plunge back into sex star status	
	the mammoth virgin in Athens or Nashville her hugely plated body dress Fort Knox
answering armswing of the moon ink ocean green scope	
	sampling *of mass* genetic *destruction* algorithm *weapons* recombine
ghost nets hollow the sea Occidio pink acid cloud	
	Sukey and Noose get it on—— no more fairy thorn
the nectar thus freed malarial pool leprosarial pox scrotal basketballs	
	hand to elbow and slate write erase write erase

tactician's dream logistician's nightmare incapable silk underpants between them	
	both the *Half-Life* and *Quake* game engines may be used in this way
put out the all-seeing eye yours mine deputized counter	
	let through the crystal the changing state selected by collapse
pulverized by Desert Shield the desert's shield of pebbles that had held down pillar billow plume	
	naked eye the Beehive a dim mist on a clear night
cipher *sifr* 0 ease and flow 1 2 3 apricot albricoque *al-birquq*	
	once met once they have met spatial separation does not divide them

To forget what has happened is a sacrament, an access
of power: the furor of these bronze leaves helpless to surround
a shrieking

ball of birdsong
gathered underneath towering
cauldrons of gold.

For nothing do you grieve. They twitter, the sound
careening like curraghs on unnavigable water. *Nothing.*
Clamor. The wind dies down. Memory

gone
visibly burning in the gold sea of the air,
cinders drifting on the black gold of the ground.

"Appearances do not deceive, if there are enough of them,"
Laura Riding, *Anarchism*.
A fact

is a failure of two things to be identical. That's a fact!
There is the freedom, moodiness,
of the body—

only my left foot
droops toward the other when, lying on
my back, mute memory

possesses me
inside its neural splash; whereas
the mind of the mystics is ever

prompt & practical. Bond-slaves of the normal,
they.
"I will follow my nose,"

they say and ride out laughing—
"No, I will retrace
my steps."

Always that note.
"It pleased not
my

lord abbot, this
lightness in
me."

ZONE MOAT ELSE

0

Sand was a gourd fanatic
and she played

      a glass

marimba.

1

Harry Soot loved to listen.

0

When Sand shook,
          a green ribbon of rainsound
rose and fell in the air,

          and when she let her mallet
fall, the palest of violets, a screen of violet
          silver unscrolled.

          1

          Soot ground his keys
                    in his pocket,
defacing his MetroCard.

0

Should Sand sing,

1

Harry felt himself leaning over a piano
          loosening his tie. As he reached out
his hand, it was as if the inside of seventeen
stretched balloons expanded past ivory,
past gray, past transparence. A single spot,
hung from the chrome scaffolding, bore
          down
on the hoof of his nail.

0

Sand had a wardrobe
made of twirlies.

     1

     Harry Soot
     tried to find a center. Beneath or beyond.
     A point to yield or resist.
     Liquefaction of furbelows.
     Buglebead ballast. Contour cups
       of constructed silk.
     A skein that flung itself into a cusp of droplets.

1

Harry Soot was a handsome man,
woody and gaunt.
A blue-eyed boy.

0

Sand well Sand was hard to say.
Some saw horns. Some saw
    slidebars. All
saw pointers
    but acknowledged them diversions.
A dragon, perhaps.

                    Or a dragon

    meditation?

0

Sand panned speed. Languid was she. Oh seeming fast, fine foil for
de . . . lay, lo, slow. Some slipp . . . age, she . . .

1

He, Harry, hurried, harried host.

0

Sand's similarity to scarabs?
Or a *rosa dolorosa*, every petal
thorned? Or swallows up close.
"The tail is forked and as elegant
as a trout's, but more attenuated,
just short of baroque," says the
naturist. I quote.

1

Harry succinct long gone
to the lake with his tackle
looking for lily berries,
looking for blue pearls. Water
holds his eyes. A silver weir.

0

Sand incessantly beckoning. Sandpipers
scurry to erase the loss of their faint
print at the foaming margin.

1

Watch Harry put a toe in.

1

Harry Soot,
unclear, of course, about fire.
        How original, originating,
it really was—
        Forests aflame. Resinous clubs.
In the dark paneled reading room,
a green shade.

        0

        Sand, a cat's cradle fan, and economic.
        Her shave and a haircut, fifteen cents;
        her Oceania nodes of knot
                remembered navigation;
        her numerous fingers interlaced
        with gloves—made of holes—slipped
        successfully over;
                her mediumistic con
        in the dark apparatus, all one, all
        the same nano-rope. This point
        escaped Harry. Harry preferred Ouija
        wavering words, reassured
        by Ouija jerk.

1

Harry is no fool. Harry Soot is shrewd.
Harry has allergies and moods.
Harry lies—he can't
                              help it.
Harry has structure—genes and grammar.
Harry is a detective, but he can't find
    an answer. Harry is violent
and violently quiet;

    01000011

    Sand is sand.

0

Sand insinuated herself. ZaumZoom in,
she has gone ahead. ZoomTzim out,
    she is not behind. To hear,
in her gourd, her mallet-fall, a relation to
    emptiness, finest gauze, so finely
        woven even the strands
            appear to disappear.

        1

        Harry Soot believes he is watching.
        Harry thinks he is in Times Square.
        He is. She is not.

0

Twirly languid blue-eyed blue pearls clearly not Sand.
Down on the fourth harmonic she simply singly for a second
stood, so symmetric, second subsequent swiftly sliding side-
riding slamjamming shivering switching—

1

Soot calls it "searching."

0

Sand sings *Nessun dorma* long summer
afternoons in the music room. Heavy red
curtains, gilded chairs, portraits of dead
children. Sand in a window seat
looking out on roses;

1

       Harry Soot in a seersucker suit
       at the far door, arms
       raised in triumph:
       his play, his score.

0

Sand seeks the scent
                of lemon viburnum,
murmuring purple
of the ringneck doves' soft
gurgle as they walk on the wall
and their syllables spill over and
                fall
        down a column
        of slowness.
Midnight blue of Krishna's

        1

        shoes. Harry finishes up.

0

Sometimes Sand doesn't come. Fatally
    blocked.
Splurt of sign signage red/blue blood
on the grisly snow. Minutes of arc off.

    1

    Harry swims in adrenalin.

0

Sand might be getting restless.
How does Sand feel about insects
as companions? Does she take
her cue from the alkaloid plants?
What seems to Soot revenge may
seem to her survival. Or
is she incapable of refusal?

1

Soot loves Sand. Every tree,
every wall, a target inscription, pierced
by Tell's weapon. Turn me on,
the swooshing sound Soot hears Sand
murmur.

0

Hold me down, Sand prays, to dusk &
musk, purple black sheathed with frost,
the Concord grape of Krishna's shoes
           with golden tips and toes
and soles. The stars are variable sprays,
                golden geometric rays
of twisted silk. Crimson lining unfolding.
Achtung! Loose lips. Beware.

1

Here comes Soot.

0

Sand resounds as long as a whale song
passed along and around the waters
of the world. Like a motherchild pod,
she/they both threatened and succored by
the coasts. Alone in the bay, rolling over and
back beneath the moon, as

1

Harry and his cohort heave
into view, traveling in a pack,
driving them aground.

0

A housedress of dotted Swiss with a lace
collar. A curling iron, to refresh
marcelled hair. Account books with black,
placeholder ribbons. Linoleum
made to look like a brick floor. Sand
could be retro.

1

Soot in tow.

0

Sand's relation to dreams bears
repeating. Was it mentioned?

1

Not necessarily Harry's.

0

As albino cave bats who let go
of coloration, but develop keener
sensors, Sand.

     1

     Soot, who seeks to catch a falling star
     in the monitoring
     cave, evolves into colorblind.

1

Harry Soot is that kind of guy. Despite
his lust for lime, despite a savvy sense
of what goes down around such light, Harry
Soot is attached to his memory lines,
crow's feet crinkle, scar arroyos, worry
furrows, wry sag, time written in skin,
in bone, in blood. Chemical peels do not
appeal to him. Nor implant chips (wait until
he gets sick!).

    01010011

    Sand's unbelievable memory
    learned, of course,
    not lived.

0

Biocompatible glass?
          Sand looks askance.
Sand an infinite receiver—
infinitely flexible. Beyond
          flex in fact, an infinite
deceiver: Proteus at home.

          1

          Siren! Circe! screams Soot.

0

Golda called Moshe that Arab.
Golda, schoolteacher, thought
words
          warded off.
Is Golda Sand?

        1

        Is Moshe Soot?
        Is Jerusalem a mass of human names . . .

0

Is Sand (a wafer/chip good as) Gold?

1

Is Soot . . . meat?

0

Sand's never the sameness fleeter than
anything Soot could get a hand, a handle,
on. Flickery swift. And yet. One finger
brings her crashing down. Hump Dump.

1

Together again—so fast it made Soot
swoon. An arcade thrill. Cheaper than
medical or bootleg. Purer, too, potent
and hygienic. Claustrophobic—no
establishing shot. Unusually
cold—most color blocked her light.

1

Harry Soot from time to time in the market for swoon.
    Perhaps ever more often. In his dream,
just a year or two ago, he remembered edge, it being
    summoned. People who forget the art
of navigation come to believe the island has sunken;

  0

  Sand's smile at this juncture, Mona Lisan.

1

Harry Soot's grandmama, Muck Raker Ida Tar . . . .
What a falling off there.

        111111111

        Sand's gramp, grep, Pythagoras.
            She done him proud. It sims.

1

Tangy Soot. Tang-I-Bull Soot.

0

Trua-vir Sand. Liv-a-Tru Sand.
Physics: The Movie. R.I.P.,
crown assays in a bathtub,
or Galileo trekking to the far side
of the valley to touch that blue
boulder on the ridge.
And would this prove he saw
mountains on the moon in any case,
Sand asks.

0

Sand, as I said, a marimba player;

1

> Oozy Soot, Uzi Soot, born to swim,
> born to dance, to paint his face, to lay
> flowers by the dead. Soot will say,
> on any given day, born to fly,
> born to rise—born to escape.

0

Sand's whimsy and scarcity/value? Sand
paints daffodils on the deck of an aircraft
carrier, caps the age of the unknown
                    universe.

        1

        Soot is running out of numbers—not
        populace. Lively virus.

0

If a silly con were all Sand were.

1

If an ashy trash were all of Soot.

0

Sand religiously stops. And starts the next thing.

1

Bluesy Soot can't conclude.

ZONE DUNGEON BODY

Just a stone barn
and Rodney's music.
There are numbers hidden
in his music, Rodney
told me: "33"
is prominent in this song,
but by way of letters,
you wouldn't hear it—

you couldn't even
figure it out, unless you
were told about it.
And about the b-flat for Barbara
—the song *was* for Barbara,
instead of just doing
that Tennyson poem—
Barbara was sick

and wouldn't get well.
But she did get well.
Not because of the song.
Rodney doesn't put
the numbers in
anymore. He says they tend
to take over.
He uses "forms"

more than he did, the line
written and not touched after,
only filled. The whole
copied, then taken apart
to copy the parts.
The b-flat was used
for "I," or "me," when the singer
sang it. But the engineer

mixed it funny, putting down
the piano entirely
when the voice appeared.
Rodney says,
that wasn't
what he meant, but you can't
be everywhere
—singers, engineers—

and he's never met
a copyist he'd trust.
He's not at all
distrustful. He's always
laughing—
always eating, thin
as a stick.
If there's even a hint

of seriousness
in the joke
you tell, he answers
you—he is grave, he loves
the barn,
or
   . . . did, back
then; I mean, he did.

About everything, in fact, they were wrong,
the Old Masters. Nothing is happening, then
—except them, the Old Masters. They are happening

when they see someone falling and someone else not
falling, framed by them with a costly ship,
or game, or horse's ass. When they see everyone

falling, in anyone falling, then they are not
Masters anymore—but men, who repent
their mastery, want to foreswear it,

but can't. Unmastered, they paint master
work: they take suffering and make it
dangle, broken-winged, treed, becalmed.

ABSINTHE 1: /

I . . . I . . . say it. Say *I. I* cannot deflect
the stagger in my limbs when the voice
that mounts me breaks; or before

possession takes, the pall of cool
and ragged darkness—leg rooting to
the ground, numbness thinning out

your mind: the descending *loa* will
accept your body, as her own, *in* her own
time. Erzulie comes—to stake

her claim: you coo, you sway, you play
for hours; then, crumpling, fade. Betrayed,
her burning tears scald your skin.

Salt petals blossom out of absinthe,
yellow bloom from a green
liquor, chlorate iron, potassium. All things,
their origins, Abyss, Abyssinian
Great Depression where rift
zones meet: before Aksum,
before Sheba, the trail blazed ten-thousand
feet, six days—six nights—to reach
the fossil lake, trekking by moonlight. Even
mules freeze, on the high plain at Makale, before
the way falls off, plunging, woods of wild
olive, candelabra euphorbia, canyon
so narrow, camels loping down
shove to their death
the laden ones, climbing.
At the foot of the escarpment,
monochrome, burning floors of salt.
Salt glitters in brine pools.
Rising from the flats, ziggurats of salt,
strange formations, turquoise, sterile.
Hungering, they come
with whitened lips, hooded eyes.
Salt grates underfoot.
Salt for gold. Salt for slaves.
Salt for salt. She was warned,
Look not behind—
In whose name did she look back?

"What I feel when I'm playing guitar
is completely cold and crazy. It's a test
just to see how far I can relax
into the cold wave of a note.
I never tire
of the solitary E . . . . "

The Red Queen straddles her throne.
Strapped to her head, liquid
crystal numerals
enforce or reprieve. What I feel
is completely cold and crazy.
It's a test. I never tire.

When dusk had drawn off
the constant shimmer of day,
when I stopped moving
and stood beneath the cliff,
trembling, eager, she
entreated me—

                small,
pied, nuzzling me;
booted, turning, leaping
to her back, I gouged, I drove
her with my lash,
where she could not go,
up the mountain.

At night, the mountain breathes,
so quiet is the air on the lower slopes.

Small dusts, returned
to their grooved bed in the dune;

debris of thistle sunk back
on the sand; dander of the animals

nestled in their shag: so quiet
has the air become, on the lower slopes,

only the shadow of a human
falls and rises on the rocks.

Guardians of the Sanctuary, Anchoress, *Furies*,
whose sound is this hissing rope, the sea,
I have lifted the sand, slept
in the dead
roots of the thorn and come before
you, Bat-Winged Ones,
with nothing but my skin,
stretched on its drum,
and one saying,
Simone's,

> *emotion*
> *that does not reach its object is the same*
> *as not loving*

By my cumbersome
tongue, mis-
namer of evil, and by these crusts of salt rising
like islands,
be moved, be moved. How many
are lost, *how many*
you have lost,

unknown. Unknown.

Are you offended,
so many—

the first

Breathe, my comforters said to me.
Gird yourself. Breathe.
And to these I said nothing.
The garden lost me.
I am ecstasy—I am no escape,
I am a mouth gaping
in the marketplace.

c. 717 to 801

Stolen as a child and sold into slavery.
Upon gaining her freedom, she retired
to a life of seclusion and celibacy.
First in the desert and then in Basra.

Lalla, we walk naked through the streets—Sibyl
taunted still by boys in the Square where she hangs
in a cage, hangs in my ear—I can't shake her
from my head, Σιβυλλα
     τι Θελεις
         (Sibyl
    what do you want?)

αποΘανειν Θελω
(I want to die.)

To refuse to choose,
or to neglect

to do so: the mother of Colette
turning in her garden, garden of earth,

delight: Sido, alone by the moon
waiting for a century

plant to bloom cannot spare her daughter.
Not even a moment. Cannot tear,

from the skim and pour of waiting,
rough, edged, time—so

offering
abyss. And Colette took up this

bread, which was black,
and spat back at Lord Death

the red
pomegranate drops.

In this desert, glass
turns
perfect. All

harshness, raining on it,
grinds away
every jag and nodule;

none of it is blank.
As it ages, it
purples;

even the black,
volcanic glass, conchoidal,
sharp, eventually

dissolves,
becoming as deep
a pool

as a pupil opening
into
an iris.

This is the Showing,
the dream
of being fed. Fed in an attic

in front of a window—
"trees lay bare
. . . in the cold air filled

with sunshine . . . . "
Lifted
from a ditch, Julian of Norwich,

her fourteenth
Revelation, found only
in the Long Book.

A window with shutters,
inner and outer, hanging vines
grieving its light.

Fed real bread.

Though it smiled,
the face was grave and slowly
turning, a great gondola flower.

Close your eyes. Shut them. Try.
They are open on both sides.

a spectre, black in the spotlight
on a hub of white cubes
spirals to the floor, sliding bare soles on the floor—

now one, with her company, hands braced,
legs flexed, wound like vines, or roots drawing
from the ground, molting

dance. None
to remember her, thrown off her axis, the arch of her fall
extended, ridden down, perilous

recovery, slowly
cantered
and turned, reversed and turned, reversing and turning . . .

On the floor of the forest, moments, expanded, aqueous, dreamlike,
can't be distinguished from endless duration. A woman

whose daughter, enticed by the dancer, once half-stood in her wheelchair—
knew, what happens happens once, if it enters that trap, door

where the mind careens toward the brain, closing in, never touching. A wheel
of lemon spurts from the knife, peels from the knife

thinner and thinner and drowns in a glass, spreading light, gold
spooks of it wobbling in soft ovals, the ferns, the root trunks rolling it, on

and on, on the vegetable floor where all decays and feeds the sea in the forest
virgin. A buried treasure, a coffer of turquoise, a rusted

trunk: an injured girl, whose mother said *it is enough*
to happen once; who said *it has happened,* if never again all is changed

here, on the ignorant floor with no way to tell time, only some bi-valve
pause then pull, where the knife as it falls stains the sea

in *la flor.* One breach bleeds forever here where the mind, conformed
to the sea, dissolves its lore. My buried treasure, my dark loam, my lost

trunk. Whose mother said, all has changed for us now.
And for my daughter. *Thanks be. Thank you all—*

Whose mother spoke to the room full of dancers, the shunning
eyes. *Thanks be to you all—for she stands. For he has seen her.*

ZONE RAMPART LOGIC

the mind distressed
disoriented dispossessed
far from the nature

"of a clear and equal glass"
seeking anew a new
co-creation

pact finds instead
a make-up mirror
to signal with or shatter

in a funk upon discovering
it *likes* electric sheep
to sleep on and keep

up with not count a kind
of company or off
on its own (its own!) body

slalom total touch re-
currently inclining
crossing to one

voice more than another
like a small creek that stays clear
through numerousness finding

steering by the falling
feel of wavelet speech re-making
(entirely) the shore

and to his *Abundance* Theorem

> particular thanks for showing Rule-governed systems are
> richer than even
>> can be described or defined, exhaustively at one
> time, so always

nougats to be made that can't
be toothed—or dis-toothed—*within* the Rule

> but that will be stickily true, nonetheless;
> a caution
>> one would think on attempts to pre-empt
>> tasty discussions, especially ones—like ours—self-

enunciations; a caution against
attempts to represent *entirety,* descending from there

> to q.e.d., as if
> one were handling truffles,
>> or trifles, in some counter-
>> game; as if corruption

and abundance itself weren't, are, *is* the same . . .

−   entropy

()

+   *decrease* of entropy

(())

−   compensated decrease of entropy

((()))

+   *uncompensated* decrease of entropy

(((())))

−   impossibility of uncompensated decrease of entropy

((((()))))

+   *reduced impossibility* of uncompensated decrease of entropy

(((((())))))

Im P robability ? 0 − + ??

−

()
+

(())

−

((()))
+

(((())))

−

((((()))))
+

(((((())))))

? 0 − + ??

E.D.: *Tell all the truth, but tell it slant . . .*

---

[1]Josiah Willard Gibbs (1839-1903), mathematical physicist, although a taciturn man, at one point asks whether there could be a "reduced impossibility of uncompensated decrease of entropy." The phrase made me laugh—the reversing polarities of the concepts, as the string unwound, seemed to cry out for more intuitive expression. Entropy had primarily negative connotations in the 19th century, but in the 20th as information-measure, shifted polarity *within* itself, bringing another twist to the now-you-see-it, now-you-don't quality of deeply nested statements. I gave Emily Dickinson the last word and in the title term, "Gibbous," refer to her, the moon, Gibbs, and those nesting parentheses all at once: "more than half but less than fully illuminated."

Every bit
lies on the border of three countries,
is a 3-country corner.

Swamp as it stands
between the land and the water, delta drained by a river-
tree, water/water-shed.

Properties of parts?
Or their articulation: Eiffel Tower
airy strong, keys of strength in the branch points.

Worn away, like coral,
like reef.
So

entirely worn
that body vanishes, all innerness outerness: rules
invent this

on the plane, in space.
" . . . not want to waste any data,
plotted all we had.

Distressing. Our eyes—
we found it hard to discriminate
landscapes we knew

to be significantly different . . . . We should
have remembered . . . to
assess

motion, one needs rest . . . one needs that standard
and the same is true of roughness."
Every bit lies on 3 frontiers:

on the banks of the branchy Bronchiole,
the swollen Artery,
and that bluest, darkest river, Vein.

pebbles begin;

then end,
at the ångstrom level—

where geography stops, our galaxy

Milk, attacked, attracted by,
the Virgo cluster;

where geography stops, each hour, again,

a Millennium
byte baptized War, where

the shot, all

gore—or
image—reel

three sheets to the wind

Never mind that the watch failed to summon,
or did sound, unheard. Dawn,

itself, streak after streak in the big windows, could not
pry open our dream. The bird

squawking at night, urgent shadows
bats made in the grass, never entered our sleep.

At noon, dragged out, unsteady—puppets hung on a high hill
drinking sunshine. Clear

our flight. Tender, prolonged, taking leave
in the laden, cold, Canadian air.

Flexing their branches, flowers awaken,
absorb energy

to die. Digits throb
red alert. Minutes speed forward only to spread

apart . . . in long moments . . .
miles to go

gone. The sun seeking ship
foundered, fallen. Done. Down.

ZONE MOTE ELSE

waves

    making the stream move back and   forth as it moves

      &
up
    down

        circling

            in

        space

    streaming

space

    moving at thespeed light light
          light dr
          light   ifts
            light
              drifts

                light

     is

what

                cannotbe

                                hurried . . . hurriedcannot
                                        behurried

If 1 is *unio*
and 2 di-lemma,
if 3 is a witness, or his testimony,
and 4 the quartet, the quire, the square,

who is
5 . . . . . and can I
recognize her by the way she talks
or only by the cones of history

pouring through her, she herself
the X-ray eyes, the Palomar
mirror, central
dissolver who nullifies

size-meaning in one smooth motion
of her telescopic barrel
centered
in a truss (the womb was a truss and the arms

of her slight mother, so light
in their touch so definite, swift as quick skies in Northern
summer
clouding and lifting, a soft

lilt

and around it, ferocious

self-completing
sentences
exerting control,

       who

like a globe-
or loganberry-flower or fingered hand
growing out of its wrist

is formed

like this (quincunxial
net, pentagonal,
❀

ago i.go   to Vega Virgo   goto

        leavethe   islandarmspiralbending   forwardslung
i.cross.i
            come.until.it

                        -asters

aplesia.silvery cones
            of the slide : a stricter palette for a unified
                    design

finest   goldwiretwisted in   flyingsunlight
        bobbing leaves with silverfoil   beneath

                reap.repeat   reap.repeat

tine eye twist in templebone

a disaster a pilaster and a jailmeister play
pool.littlegreen willytadpoles

jasper
travertine gate non.enough
nenny

whatit scenes

<table>
<tr>
<td>

my mother killed by lightning

[

in] a high-risk environment of

air

vision

millions of years

each stone   I carve . . .   [I] convolve
with mathematical ideas . . .   the form

that no one
has ever felt

</td>
<td>

through a development
of consciousness I detached myself from
spontaneous
      expression . . . turned to . . . more

systematic

electricity water dust and chips

that calls for
      special
        breathing
apparatus
hearing protection
body
     armor . . . insulation . . . I
undo by violence   air
hammers
carbide cutters diamond corers saws
hydraulic rams gantry cranes

of geologic material-forming processes

walked around or

crawled through

</td>
</tr>
</table>

                        rules calculate
                and generate the work
Bense and Barbaud changed my thinking

for each Laserglyph a random selection

                        4

—from this repertoire of 23,040
                diagonal-paths
        in a 6-d hypercube—

flattened into visibility :
a 2-d sign of great spatial ambiguity

                        animation
hangs onscreen

        bring light
        into the body and hold it
        there

                I have one now
                        one billion years old
                waiting

toward a rational construction

                        day after day
        a different image
                        appears

seeing is forgetting the name
        of what you see

                very slow-motion
flicker

        figurine tokens to stylized text :
        the *evolution* of notation . . .
                turning . . .
                back

I learn my form my (subtractive) form

    from computed information

        like learning a piece of
music by heart or a choreographic
      sequence

treading a wave

the heaviest-duty black industrial
enamel I could find
      toxic colloidal gunk
broken up with red wine
India ink
sludge from the bottom of the brush jar

created this very lyrical and delicate

      image landscape on the surface
a performance so convincing people
swear

        it is photography

    so it was self-organizing?

  totally
    well

        I finally learned to see
beyond the retinal
    experience

    eighty-five percent—
      which I liked

a scanner starts at the beginning
and moves ever so slowly
to the end of the scan
it may take 30 seconds or so

this is just what the Quick-TimeVR
movies do but on a horizontal plane

you join

the ends so you just turn centered
in an infinite image loop
onscreen

somebody will shoot all the backgrounds
somebody will shoot all the people

all the people on blue-screen   tribal   *mask*   zone

somebody will shoot all the clouds   historical   *mirror*   zone
you're going to replace into the sky

    numerical   *image*   zone

the compositor composits it all

output to
whatever format you want
video DV film whatever

Quick-Time Virtual Reality

                    to break down or bring out
                        the scanner pieces

like turning an urn
photographing all sides

                    so they become an event

use a cursor to travel around it or you can
be   inside
take your pick

                            QTVR space
                        scanner space

the original panorama has a very quiet

quality about it because the beginning
and the end
join seamlessly

                                I work   inside
                                    "the urn"
                                it seems like reality to me

    flesh
    format

                                          physical   presence   luminosity
                                                  wanting to touch

                                please don't touch
                                almost any
                                                photographic paper will
                                fingerprint if you touch

huge failure rate
which I now take for granted
                        I can work
with some accident
but I still have a great many disasters
usually through pushing something
too far

                        the air   lives

                by turning green
            not struck from stones
not blossoming out of twigs   within the wind a little wind
                                                    within the light a greater light
                                                        Ignota Lingua
not rooted
in a power to beget
                        H. of B.
                                                greenness not a color

        complication of the process
                                                longwinded
                                                enumeration

                                                        flax to linen rag to paper

Graces flying from the Hunter
pass the woman weeding flax

who detains him

whiling away the fatal hour

with the tedious story

distracting aggressor
ghosts all night until the cock crew

thrown in the ditch
pulled out by the hair
skinned heckled broken scorched
washed in lyes worried

to pulp

as flax is hackled with a comb of thorns
grapes are ripped from stalks
with the comb of the fingers

I have not tortured
the plants
nor have I shoveled them into the oven

buried blue-eyed flowering plucked root
& branch retted soaked to partial rotting
scorched over fire bound battered dressed
rippled with hackle combs and thorns
drawn fiber spun thread woven *linen*
bleached on grass pierced needles sewn
shirt worn to rag rent drowned calendered
dried to paper   written on

It is another who did this
and brought them to me

I ate innocently

spoken to the loaf

[goddess]
　　Reply seized [the divine son] Death

　　　　　　　　　　　to cut
　　　　winnow roast and scatter　　for birds to eat to break the spell
　　　　　　　　　　　　　　　　scattered not sown　　older
　　　　　　　　　　　　　　　　than bread

　　　　　　　　　　　　　　　　a feast "Denial"
　　　　　　　　　　　　　　　　in the month Denial
　　　　　　　　rent to pieces　　at which all dogs
　　　　　　　　by "dogs"　　　　met in the market are killed
　　　　　　　　harvesters
　　　　　　　　masquerade

　　　passion of the flax　　　　　　　　to seem to refer not to divinized
　　　　　　　　　　　　　　　　barley of Babylonia
　　　　　　　　　　　　　　　　　　nor sacred green ear of Eleusis
　　　　　　　　　　　　　　　　　　　but the child born

　　　　　　　　　　　　　　　　　House of Bread Beth-Lehem

seven virgin disciples
　　whose flesh shines during torture
as white as the shining

　　　　　　　　silvery

　　　　　　　　　　　　　　　　fiber of the flax

　　　　　　　　silver

　　　　　　　　　　　　　　　　grain

photochemicals flood the emulsion
acidic and basic waves compete on film
      to fix
            or strip suspended
          silver

        palette of stained glass
            childhood
       window
light as it falls is winnowed plucked
    by the Polaroid

image that records pure saturated light   what language do you write in

                                     C++

                              do you work in the Mac or PC world

                              the SGI world
   I have also been making photograms   which is doing so poorly
      the paper negatives are striking   Unix and SGI are my loves
    in their rich luxurious warm blacks

   I teach compositing and effects
using Flame
and Flint
applications by Discrete Logic

you've got purists to whom
algorithmic art
is the only way to go
but then who's to say that's right

I find myself kind of alone at the Academy
they're into turning out people
who can get jobs
in the animation industry

Genetic Brushes
an evolutionary model where you could
breed two brushes together
they would make a whole new brush

brush over the entire image algorithmically
no human
intervention other than setting
the basic parameters

brush size color angle etc.
calculated
based on info from the image
whether it was luminance
or hue   or . . .

Denial
a bed of slender
reeds

living on light

(. . . to come

numerical   *image*   zone

at the bottom of the food chain
underwater

(. . . to come

(. . . to come

of slipping glimpse

a realm

That first fact that a Star
Appears fixed, a *Nail*
Of the North, a Sky
Hole to hold Earth axle—
Spin-steer, Lodestar

Cynosura.

Pole Star to the Akkadai,
Spinning Girl,
Girl with a Shuttle in China.
Vega in Lyra—tortoise shell—
Solar System flying toward her.

13 millennia on,

Once again Vega Pole Star—
Will on Earth any (be to) see her?
13 millennia back, bards, bull-
Jumpers, cats, the new
Great Lakes, blue-eyed flax.

Epigraph

For the Birds: John Cage in Conversation with Daniel Charles. Boston: Marion Boyars, 1981, cited by Joan Retallack on p. 261 of *The Poethical Wager,* University of California Press, 2003. On p. 258 of the same volume, Retallack glosses the quotation:

"These words may not be precisely John Cage's at all. They are taken from his conversations with Daniel Charles, which have, as text, an odd history. *For the Birds* is an English translation of a French transcription of interviews taped in English. The tapes were lost before they could be transcribed directly into English, and Cage himself said he didn't recognize much of the voiced labeled "J.C." at the end of all that. So the puzzling over these words is not so much trying to get at what was originally said, which is clearly irrecoverable, as trying to make useful meaning of words that have the attraction of initiating a process of "not-knowing," opening an edge in the mind, beyond which lie things not thought of before. This is an exhilarating notion, even if self-delusory. It has to do with the structure of the reading experience, the structure of language itself."

Survey, p. 7

Deep Field: In 1995 the Hubble Space Telescope was pointed at the same bit of sky for 10 days in a row. The resulting image is known as the Hubble Deep Field. It "strongly suggest[s] that every quarter square degree of the sky—an area about the same size as the disk of a full moon—encompasses millions of galaxies." *The Sciences* 40, 2000, p. 33.

Dominance of dark:

". . . about 95 percent of the universe is made up of stuff that workers have yet to fully identify. Another 4 percent is . . . clouds of extremely hot hydrogen and helium gas . . . . Nearly half of 1 percent is made up of neutrinos left over from the big bang. That leaves just 0.5 percent for the material locked up in stars—all the stars, in all the galaxies. And the atoms that have been formed since the big bang in the heart of stars and the aftermath of supernovas . . . everything else in the periodic table save hydrogen and helium, all that accounts for just two parts in 10,000 of the bulk of the universe.

"It is humbling to discover that the chemical elements we are made of account for so little of the composition of the universe. Even the stars themselves pale in significance beside the dark matter and dark energy that make up the 'real' universe. In fact, it would not be far-fetched to say that the billions upon billions of stars and the galaxies that populate what is usually thought of as the universe are insubstantial." *The Sciences* 40, 2000, p. 37.

Sloan Survey at Sunspot: "More recently, another study of the heavens, the Sloan Digital Sky Survey at the Apache Point Observatory in Sunspot, New Mexico, has discovered . . . that the very idea of individual galaxies may be an illusion— . . . galaxies are . . . distant points of color that decorate a much larger, though unseen, web." *The Sciences* 40, 2000, p. 33.

War Day, p. 9

"no woman no cry": Bob Marley song; its refrain, "no woman, no cry," woman, don't cry. From "No Woman No Cry," words and music by Vincent Ford, copyright © 1974 Fifty-Six Hope Road Music, Ltd., Odnil Music, Ltd., and Blue Mountain Music, Ltd.

Plum Creek: On the Banks of Plum Creek by Laura Ingalls Wilder, one of her *Little House on the Prairie* series of children's books.

Plum Island: Our bio-weapons of mass destruction lab, Plum Island is located between Long Island and Connecticut.

spent fuel rocks: Uranium to be reprocessed, used to irradiate food.

ember-eyed stranger: Shiva, god of death. His long black curly hair is used to modulate divine forces to secular ones, for instance the Milky Way to the Ganges, in Hindu myth.

mammoth virgin: Athena at the Parthenon, originally covered in gold.

ghost nets: Abandoned by industrial fishing factories, ghost nets drift through the ocean killing wildlife.

Occidio: Latin for slaughter, massacre. Name of a global warming sound and video installation: http://www.research.umbc.edu/~nohe/OCCIDIO/

pink acid cloud:

> "In the event, there is no mistaking them. As the Sun dips over the horizon, a mass of tear-shaped clouds appears from nowhere. They are petrol blue and green, rimmed with vibrant pink-lurid colours that have no business in a sunset. Against the monochrome backdrop of snow and forest, they are shocking.
>
> "At 20 kilometres or more above the ground, the clouds lie far above the world's normal weather patterns. You'll find them only at the highest latitudes, like here in Swedish Lapland over the tiny, frozen town of Kiruna, 200 kilometres north of the Arctic Circle. These clouds are natural—but they are also dangerous. At the other end of the world it's clouds like these that trigger the infamous Antarctic ozone hole each southern spring."
>
> http://www.newscientist.com/hottopics/climate/climate.jsp?id=22314500 (May 31, 2004)

Sukey and Noose: English homophones for Greek ψυκη, spirit/psyche, and νους, mind.

Half-Life and *Quake:* Popular FPS (First Person Shooter) computer games that use the same engine. From the *GameSpot* review of *Quake:* "Once again, the team at Id Software has created a no-apologies, ultra-violent gorefest sure to be the new battleground of choice for single and multi-player combatants worldwide."

Beehive: constellation.

The Interior Castle, p. 13

Teresa of Avila, 1515–1582, gadabout visionary and reformer during the time of the Inquisition, "transverberated" Doctor of Theology of the Catholic Church. She finished writing *Interior Castle/The Abodes (Castillo interior/Las moradas)* in 1577.

Ballad of Sand and Harry Soot, p. 17

The Ballad of Sand and Harry Soot, a visual hypertext made with Janet Holmes, is available online at http://www.wordcircuits.com/gallery/sandsoot and on the CD included with this book.

[William] Tell's weapon: an arrow

Absinthe: The Twelve, p. 57

Absinthe: 1. green liqueur made from wormwood 2. plant, wormwood. Wormwood and sagebrush belong to the genus *Artemisia*. According to the Gary Snyder poem, "Earrings Dangling and Miles of Desert": "Artemisia is worldwide—thirty species in Japan alone. It's the mugwort and moxa of China. Wormwood is sacred to Artemis. Narrow leaves glow silver in her moonlight—"

I: Maya Deren (born Eleanora Derenkovskaya), 1917–1961, related her experience of possession by Erzulie, one of the Voudoun Deities known as *loa*, in the "White Darkness" chapter of her book, *Divine Horsemen: The Living Gods of Haiti.*

Pillar: Salt Pillar and Sheba are Biblical figures. "[T]he ages-old trail from the Ethiopian highlands into the depths of the Danakil Depression . . . was well established at the time of the very first Ethiopian empire, Aksum, which Third Century sources mention in the same breath with Rome, Persia, and China." *Salt the Mysterious Necessity,* Dow Chemical Company, 1972.

Patti: Patti Smith, 1946–, poet, composer, actress.

Apollinaria-Dorotheus: The woman Apollinaria (550–600, or d. 470?) took the male name Dorotheus to survive as a hermit in the Syrian desert.

Winged Goddesses with Serpentine Hair: The Furies (Erinyes) appear in Aeschylus' *Eumenides* (Well-Meaning Ones/Gracious Ones). There Athena flatteringly re-names them, in an attempt to win them over (to support the state).

The italicized phrase is Simone Weil's. Weil, a French philosopher and mystic, lived from 1909–1943.

Rabi'a: Rabi'a al-'Adawiyya, or Rabi'a of Basra, an 8th-century Sufi saint. *Lalla:* In Hindi, *Lal Ded* (Grandmother Lal) and in Sanskrit, *Lalleshwari* (Lalla the yogini)—a 14th century Kashmiri mystic. Thanks to Dorothy Disse for Other Women's Voices: http://home.infionline.net/~ddisse/. *Sybil:* The Cumaean Sibyl as described by Petronius appears in the epigraph to T. S. Eliot's "The Waste Land."

Colette: Sidonie Gabrielle Colette, 1873–1954, French novelist; Sido, her mother.

Amma: Early Christians, precursors of monasticism, inhabited the deserts of the Middle East from the end of the second century CE onwards. Their stories, rules, and traditions are codified as the Sayings or teachings of the Desert Fathers, often transmitted in the form, "Abba Antony said," "Abba Evagrius said," and so on. The few women were called Amma, as in "Amma Theodora asked." Amma is also used for an abbess or spiritual mother.

Enormous Washerwomen on Stilts: "trees lay bare...": Simone Weil, from the so-called Prologue, found after her death on two loose sheets in a late London–America journal. Presumably written in Marseilles, it was published in *La Connaissance surnaturelle. Julian of Norwich:* 14–15th century English anchoress (solitary) who lived in a period of rival Popes and Black Death. Her book, *Showings,* or *A Book of Showings to the Anchoress Julian of Norwich*, was composed in both a short and long form. The Bread and Puppet street theater performance characters include many on stilts as well as enormous washerwomen on the ground.

Dancer: Doris Humphrey, 1895–1958, pioneering dancer and choreographer, wrote *The Art of Making Dances.*

Prisoner in the Tower, p. 75

Eric McLuhan:

"For centuries, Francis Bacon has been revered as a philosopher and as the founder of modern science—an honour which would have baffled him." McLuhan quotes Bacon: "For the mind of man is far from the nature of a clear and equal glass, wherein the beams of things should reflect according to their true incidence; nay, it is rather like an enchanted glass, full of superstition and imposture, if it be not delivered and reduced. For this purpose, let us consider the false appearances that are imposed upon us by the general nature of the mind . . . Let us consider again the false appearances imposed upon us by every man's own individual nature and custom . . . And lastly let us consider the false appearances that are imposed upon us by words . . . and although we think we govern our words . . . yet certain it is that words, as a Tartar's bow, do shoot back upon the understanding of the wisest, and mightily entangle and pervert the judgment."   http://www.chass.utoronto.ca/mcluhan-studies/v1_iss4/1_4art1.htm

To Gödel, p. 77

Kurt Gödel, 1906–1978, Austrian logician, famed for his Incompleteness Theorem, renamed here Abundance. The following is quoted from Jones and Wilson, *An Incomplete Education,* 1987, 1995:

"In 1931, the Czech-born mathematician Kurt Gödel demonstrated that within any given branch of mathematics, there would always be some propositions that couldn't be proven either true or false using the rules and axioms . . . of that mathematical branch itself. You might be able to prove every conceivable statement about numbers within a system by going *outside* the system in order to come up with new rules and axioms, but by doing so you'll only create a larger system with its own unprovable statements. The implication is that *all* logical systems of any complexity are, by definition, incomplete; each of them contains, at any given time, more true statements than it can possibly prove according to its own defining set of rules."

Islands (Invaginated by Saltwater . . .), p. 79
The quote (somewhat adapted) is from Benoit Mandelbrot's *The Fractal Geometry of Nature*, 1983, p. C12.

Prisoner in the Cave, p. 82
The Cave as a space of duped knowers who take reflections for reality, shadows for bodies, goes back at least as far as Plato's *Symposium*. Ice Age caves, by contrast, like those in Spain and Southern France, seem to be inner sancta, "true" locations of reality or evocative locations of knowledge and simulation.

21st-century Caves [Computed Automated Virtual Environments] create virtual reality spaces in which participants, using special goggles and wands, can become immersed. The Matrix, in the movie by the Wachowski Brothers, is a kind of cave in this tradition.

The Icarian projects, space shuttles Columbia (and Challenger), are referred to at the end of this poem.

electrical disturbances . . . , p. 85
According to current physics, the speed of light is a constant, so it can neither slow nor hurry.

slippingglimpse, p. 91
slippingglimpse, a 10-part interactive generative Flash poem combining video and the text of this poem, made in collaboration with Cynthia Lawson Jaramillo and Paul Ryan, is online at http://slippingglimpse.org and on the CD included with this book. It was introduced at e-Poetry 2007 (Paris) in May 2007. In this work, the ocean videos 'read' the poem-text using motion capture coding that assigns the text locations of movement in the water. In turn, the poem-text 'reads' image/capture technologies by sampling and recombining the words of visual artists who describe their use of digital techniques; it then explores older capture technologies, such as harvesting plants for food and flax for paper. Completing the round-robin reading loop, image capture videography 'reads' the water, reading for and enhancing water flow patterns (chreods) to which dynamical systems return even as they continuously change. Chreods, as part of catastrophe theory, were developed by the mathematician René Thom. They provide a language for transition

that coordinates all the systems controlling transformation and were regarded by Thom as 'words' in a multi-dimensional, environmental language.

The language of "slippingglimpse" comes in part from sampling, recombining, even quoting verbatim, phrases from articles by Helaman Ferguson, Manfred Mohr, and Paul Fishwick in *YLEM: Artists Using Science and Technology*, no. 10, vol. 22, September–October 2002, "Art and Programming"; and also phrases from interviews of Marius Johnston, David Berg, Frances Dose, and Susan Rankaitis by Loren Means, as well as articles by Ellen Carey and Jon Lybrook in *YLEM: Artists Using Science and Technology*, double issue no. 4 and 6, volume 22, March–June 2002, "Photo-based Experimental Work." Thanks also to Ruth Eckland for an YLEM Forum program note in that issue, and particular thanks to David Berg for expressing his wish to "create a realm of slipping glimpse . . . ."

Bense and Barbaud: Mohr mentions German philosopher Max Bense and French composer Pierre Barbaud.

H. of B.: Hildegardis (Hildegard of Bingen), 1098–1179, among whose many accomplishments may be counted the construction of a language, *Ignota Lingua*. Hildegard celebrated *viriditas* ("greenness") throughout her songs and her prose. Scholars debate what she meant.

flax: Folkloric material is based on Robert Eisler's "The Passion of the Flax," *Folklore* 62, 114–133 (1951).

Versus Vega : Precessing, p. 101

The orientation of the Earth's rotational axis varies slowly over time, due to the pull on the swelling at the Earth's equator by the Sun and the Moon, a gyration known as precession, or precession of the equinoxes. If the earth's axis were a long pencil writing on the dome of the sky, it would seem to draw a circle every 26,000 years. This pencil points always to the North Star, which today is Polaris, a star in the handle of the Little Dipper, but 12,000 years from now will be Vega.

Versus Vega : Precessing, a visual hypertext, Hovering into Hovering, with Jason Nelson, is available online at http://www.secrettechnology.com/resident/strickland.htm or http://www.secrettechnology.com/resident/residency.htm

Since 1995 Stephanie Strickland has been equally involved with writing print and electronic poems and has created works that have won simultaneous national awards in both forms. She curated and participated in *The Brave New Word* at the Guggenheim Museum. At Georgia Tech, where she held the McEver Chair in Writing, she created, curated, and produced TechnoPoetry Festival, which brought together artists, performers, and theorists to explore writing with new technologies and the ways that translation, transliteration, and transcription are all rethought in the digital era.

Strickland's poems have appeared widely, including in *The Paris Review, Grand Street, New American Writing, Fence, Chain, American Letters & Commentary,* and in many anthologies. Her first book of poems, *Give the Body Back,* was published by the University of Missouri Press. Her second, *The Red Virgin: A Poem of Simone Weil,* was selected for the Brittingham Prize by Lisel Mueller and published by the University of Wisconsin Press. Her third, *True North,* was chosen by Barbara Guest for the Poetry Society of America's Di Castagnola Prize. It went on to win the first Ernest Sandeen Poetry Prize, chosen by John Matthias, and was published by the University of Notre Dame Press. *True North,* the hypertext, was published on disk by Eastgate Systems and awarded a *Salt Hill* Hypertext Prize. Her volume, *V: WaveSon.nets / Losing L'una* was published by Penguin and was chosen for the PSA Di Castagnola Prize by Brenda Hillman. *V* features an online component, http://vniverse.com, made with Cynthia Lawson Jaramillo.

Ahsahta Press

SAWTOOTH POETRY PRIZE SERIES

2002: Aaron McCollough, *Welkin* (Brenda Hillman, judge)

2003: Graham Foust, *Leave the Room to Itself* (Joe Wenderoth, judge)

2004: Noah Eli Gordon, *The Area of Sound Called the Subtone* (Claudia Rankine, judge)

2005: Karla Kelsey, *Knowledge, Forms, The Aviary* (Carolyn Forché, judge)

2006: Paige Ackerson-Kiely, *In No One's Land* (D. A. Powell, judge)

2007: Rusty Morrison, *the true keeps calm biding its story* (Peter Gizzi, judge)

NEW SERIES

1. Lance Phillips, *Corpus Socius*
2. Heather Sellers, *Drinking Girls and Their Dresses*
3. Lisa Fishman, *Dear, Read*
4. Peggy Hamilton, *Forbidden City*
5. Dan Beachy-Quick, *Spell*
6. Liz Waldner, *Saving the Appearances*
7. Charles O. Hartman, *Island*
8. Lance Phillips, *Cur aliquid vidi*
9. Sandra Miller, *oriflamme.*
10. Brigitte Byrd, *Fence Above the Sea*
11. Ethan Paquin, *The Violence*
12. Ed Allen, *67 Mixed Messages*
13. Brian Henry, *Quarantine*
14. Kate Greenstreet, *case sensitive*
15. Aaron McCollough, *Little Ease*
16. Susan Tichy, *Bone Pagoda*
17. Susan Briante, *Pioneers in the Study of Motion*
18. Lisa Fishman, *The Happiness Experiment*
19. Heidi Lynn Staples, *Dog Girl*
20. David Mutschlecner, *Esse*
21. Kristi Maxwell, *Realm Sixty-four*
22. G. E. Patterson, *To and From*
23. Chris Vitiello, *Irresponsibility*
24. Stephanie Strickland, *Zone : Zero*
25. Charles O. Hartman, *New and Selected Poems*

Ahsahta Press

MODERN AND CONTEMPORARY
POETRY OF THE AMERICAN WEST

Sandra Alcosser, *A Fish to Feed All Hunger*

David Axelrod, *Jerusalem of Grass*

David Baker, *Laws of the Land*

Dick Barnes, *Few and Far Between*

Conger Beasley, Jr., *Over DeSoto's Bones*

Linda Bierds, *Flights of the Harvest-Mare*

Richard Blessing, *Winter Constellations*

Boyer, Burmaster, and Trusky, eds., *The Ahsahta Anthology*

Peggy Pond Church, *New and Selected Poems*

Katharine Coles, *The One Right Touch*

Wyn Cooper, *The Country of Here Below*

Craig Cotter, *Chopstix Numbers*

Judson Crews, *The Clock of Moss*

H. L. Davis, *Selected Poems*

Susan Strayer Deal, *The Dark is a Door*

Susan Strayer Deal, *No Moving Parts*

Linda Dyer, *Fictional Teeth*

Gretel Ehrlich, *To Touch the Water*

Gary Esarey, *How Crows Talk and Willows Walk*

Julie Fay, *Portraits of Women*

Thomas Hornsby Ferril, *Anvil of Roses*

Thomas Hornsby Ferril, *Westering*

Hildegarde Flanner, *The Hearkening Eye*

Charley John Greasybear, *Songs*

Corrinne Hales, *Underground*

Hazel Hall, *Selected Poems*

Nan Hannon, *Sky River*

Gwendolen Haste, *Selected Poems*

Kevin Hearle, *Each Thing We Know Is Changed Because We Know It And Other Poems*

Sonya Hess, *Kingdom of Lost Waters*

Cynthia Hogue, *The Woman in Red*

Robert Krieger, *Headlands, Rising*

Elio Emiliano Ligi, *Disturbances*

Haniel Long, *My Seasons*

Ken McCullough, *Sycamore•Oriole*

Norman MacLeod, *Selected Poems*

Barbara Meyn, *The Abalone Heart*

David Mutschlecner, *Esse*

Dixie Partridge, *Deer in the Haystacks*

Gerrye Payne, *The Year-God*

George Perreault, *Curved Like an Eye*

Howard W. Robertson, *to the fierce guard in the Assyrian Saloon*

Leo Romero, *Agua Negra*

Leo Romero, *Going Home Away Indian*

Miriam Sagan, *The Widow's Coat*

Philip St. Clair, *At the Tent of Heaven*

Philip St. Clair, *Little-Dog-of-Iron*

Donald Schenker, *Up Here*

Gary Short, *Theory of Twilight*

D. J. Smith, *Prayers for the Dead Ventriloquist*

Richard Speakes, *Hannah's Travel*

Genevieve Taggard, *To the Natural World*

Tom Trusky, ed., *Women Poets of the West*

Marnie Walsh, *A Taste of the Knife*

Bill Witherup, *Men at Work*

Carolyne Wright, *Stealing the Children*

This book is set in Apollo MT type with Bank Gothic titles
by Ahsahta Press at Boise State University
and manufactured according to the Green Press Initiative
by Thomson-Shore, Inc.
Cover design by Quemadura.
Book design by Janet Holmes.

AHSAHTA PRESS
2008

JANET HOLMES, DIRECTOR
BREONNA KRAFFT
AMBER NELSON
DAVID SCOTT
NAOMI TARLE
ROSS HARGREAVES, INTERN